Tryouts for Ben

By
Jean M. Cogdell

Copyright © 2015 Jean M. Cogdell

All rights reserved. No part of this book may be reproduced or transmitted in any form or by any means, electronic or mechanical, including photocopying, recording, or by any information storage and retrieval system, without permission from the copyright owner.
ISBN: 978-0-9971286-0-4

DEDICATION

To my patient, loving husband and family from whom all inspiration comes. And a big thank you to all those who gave their time and expertise to help make this happen.

ACKNOWLEDGMENT

Illustrations by Ashley Bauer

This is a work of fiction. Names, characters, places and incidents either are the product of the author's imagination or are used fictitiously. Any resemblance to actual persons, living or dead, events, or locales is entirely coincidental.

CONTENTS

DEDICATION ii
ACKNOWLEDGEMENTS ii
CHAPTER 1 - MY PLAN 1
CHAPTER 2 - TRYOUTS BEGIN 7
CHAPTER 3- FLAG FOOTBALL 12
CHAPTER 4 - ICE HOCKEY 18
CHAPTER 5 - RUINED BREAKFAST 25
CHAPTER 6 - BASEBALL TRYOUTS 28
CHAPTER 7 - SOCCER FUN 35
CHAPTER 8 - BASKETBALL GIANT 39
ABOUT THE AUTHOR 49

CHAPTER 1 - MY PLAN

I dug my feet into the ground, pushed off, and flew high into the air.

My name is Benjamin Wade Marshall, and if I'm not inside playing video games, you can find me here on my swing. This is where I do my best thinking and planning.

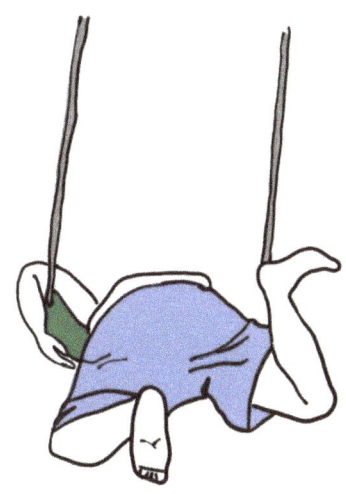

As I flew through the air, I came up with the perfect summer plan.

Play on my swing in the mornings, video games after lunch and before bed watch my favorite TV shows.

Sounds perfect, right?

Too bad my dad had other ideas.

"Ben, I've been thinking, he said.

I looked up from my plate of spaghetti and found him staring at me. Uh, oh I had a bad feeling. Dad's big smile reminded me of Roger Woodruff when he said, "Pull my finger."

I only fell for that trick once.

"Yeah, Dad?" I swallowed a big bite of noodles and focused on my half empty plate.

In times like this, best not make eye contact. I learned a long time ago, a kid never wins a staring contest, not with a smiling parent.

"Well, I thought you should try out for a team sport this summer."

I worked to swallow a mouthful of long squiggly noodles and almost choked.

After a sip of water, I tried to sound uninterested as I asked, "Which one?"

"Try out a few, see which one fits best," he said.

Dad stopped eating, leaned forward and proceeded to explain his plans for my summer. For the next few minutes, I listened in horror. He had decided I should learn to play a sport, like my big brother, Alex. A team sport. But here's the problem, I stink.

When I say I stink, I mean stink like old gym socks. Especially, the socks Alex drops all over the bedroom floor. By the end of the week, the odor is so bad our cat Tiger refuses to come in our room.

Need an example?

Let me tell you what happened one rainy day at school. The teachers herded everyone into the gym for some exercise. Most of the time, recess is my favorite part of the school day because I get to swing on the playground swings. On swings that go way higher than mine at home. But not on rainy days. That's when we *exercise* in the gym.

As I was saying, it's raining and we're stuck in the gym goofing off more than exercising. That was okay, that is until…

One of the teachers brought out a dodgeball. I hate dodgeball.

Anyone should be able to play dodgeball. Right? Wrong. That ball hit me more times than I could count.

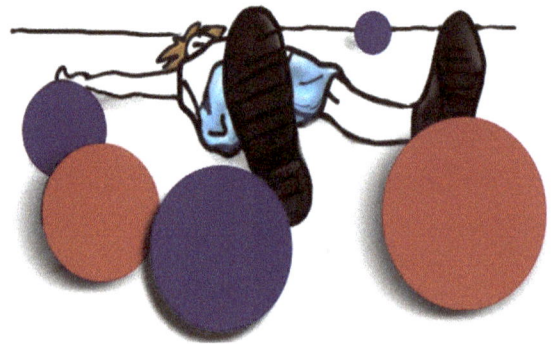

Dee Daniels, the most annoying girl in second grade, beaned me every time she got her grubby hands on a ball. She reminded me how much I didn't like girls. They giggle a lot and are just plain annoying.

After another hard bing in the middle of my back, I decided to stay down. I stared at the ceiling for a few minutes before I rolled over and crawled to the bleachers.

As I sat on the bleacher and nursed my bruised ego, I overheard a couple of teachers talking.

"Some kids at this age are a bit uncoordinated," said Mrs. Randall.

"Yes, they trip over their own feet," said Mr. Whitemore, the gym teacher.

I jumped to my feet ready to tell them both I hadn't tripped. Thank goodness the bell rang. A stampede of kids rushed for the door and the distraction saved me from detention. Mr. Whitmore is famous for handing out detentions.

I might not trip over my own feet, but, honest, I'm not good at sports.

I'm good at climbing and swinging, but sports? Nope, I don't think so. A guy knows when he's good at something and when he's not. I stink at sports, even dodgeball.

Oh yeah, there is one thing I'm good at—video games. When I'm in the middle of an epic game, I can play for hours without a break.

My dad thinks that's the problem.

He said I spend too much time alone, and playing a sport will be good for me. He's wrong. Because, no one gets hurt playing video games.

CHAPTER 2 - TRYOUTS BEGIN

The first day of summer break, I sat in the kitchen and waited until Dad finished his morning coffee.

Everyone at our house knows not to ask Dad anything before coffee. His answer is always no before coffee.

"Um, Dad, you know what? I don't think playing a sport is a good idea," I said.

Dad looked up over the top of his newspaper.

"And why is that?" he asked.

I held up my pointer finger. "One, I stink."

My middle finger popped up and joined my pointer.

"Two, I just finished second grade. If I wait until I'm in the ninth grade like Alex, I might be good at sports. Maybe even baseball."

Dad loves baseball. I thought if I mentioned his favorite sport it might buy me some time.

However, I could not see myself ever becoming a sports star. Not like my brother Alex. He pitches for his high school team and is a great player.

Positive, I'd solved my problem, I gave Dad my biggest, goofiest smile and started toward the living room. Today, I planned to make it to the next level on the World of Magic Racing.

Boy oh boy, I was wrong. My reasons didn't work, and my problems were just beginning.

Dad's voice stopped my exit.

"Not so fast!" he called out. "One, how do you know you stink? You haven't even tried. Two, waiting until high school is NOT an option, lots of kids your age play sports. And three, your mom's ready to take you to the first tryouts. Don't look as if this is the end of the world. You might even have fun."

Easy for him to say. Dad and Alex are good at everything. His plans for me might not be the end of the world, but it sounded like the end of my summer.

Mom walked to the back door and jangled her keys. "Let's go," she said.

"Now?" I gulped.

I climbed into the van, buckled up, closed my eyes and imagined I was a hostage. You know those guys on TV? A bad guy forces a good guy in a van and then drives off with him.

Yeah, that's me—the good guy—a hostage in Mom's van on the way to play with a bunch of kids I didn't know.

Don't get me wrong. I've got nothing against sports. I've gone to every one of Alex's games, and over the years, that's been a lot of baseball games. But I'm terrible at sports. Believe me, I STINK.

All the way to the park, Mom talked non-stop about something called "flag football." I'd never heard of it.

Last winter I watched a few football games on TV with Dad and Alex. I didn't see any players with flags. Another thing, the football players on TV were huge, and they still got hurt.

Look at me! I'm little. If I play football, it just might be my last day on earth.

At the park, I walked behind Mom, dragging my feet and kicking up gravel. To my left, I spotted a playground filled with swings. Did I mention I love to swing?

Mom saw me drooling and gave me her famous "Don't you dare!" scowl. Then she grabbed my hand and dragged me toward the football field.

No way out. I was doomed.

CHAPTER 3- FLAG FOOTBALL

A big, burly coach walked over, and my hand disappeared in what grownups call a "hearty handshake." Watching my hand disappear in his didn't help the butterflies in my stomach one bit.

I flexed my hand and counted my fingers. Whew! What a relief. I still had five.

The coach helped me tie on a funny looking belt with dangling ribbons. He explained those were called flags. Weird. Sounded like a game of capture the flag instead of football. Every time I moved, those ribbons felt like bugs crawling up my legs. But as long as I avoided the football, I'd be safe and so would my creepy, crawly flag belt.

TWEET! I was standing close to the Coach. When he blew his whistle, my ears almost exploded.

I slapped my hands over my ears to mute the piercing sound, turned away, and almost bumped into another kid. A girl.

Holy cow! My mouth flopped open and shut like a big fish. Girls were on this team!

Now let me say this—girls shouldn't play football. And, for sure, girls with long blond ponytails shouldn't play football. This looked like a Dee Daniels experience about to happen all over again. I backed up and decided to keep my distance from her.

The black greasepaint smeared under some of the player's eyes was a bit strange. But still I thought tryouts might go alright, that is until…

One of the big guys growled and glared at me. I stepped back stumbled and fell to the ground. This didn't seem like a very friendly game.

I'm almost embarrassed to tell you what happened. Practice did not go good, not good at all. For a no tackle game, flag football sure was a dangerous game.

I spent more time on the ground that day looking up at the sky than playing football. Did I tell you, I stink at football?

I limped to the van, positive every bone in my body was broken.

In case you ever find yourself on a football field, I've got a tip to help you survive.

Flag Football Tip: Don't get tackled, and run fast.

That night, Dad said he was proud of me, and Mom assured me nothing was broken.

"You're just sore from all the exercise," she said. "You're going to be fine."

How could she be so sure? I didn't feel fine. My eyelids felt as if weights were attached. I was so tired, I fell asleep at the dinner table. When I woke up, I had mashed potatoes on my cheek and green peas in my hair.

It was going to be a long summer.

Can somebody help me, please?

CHAPTER 4 - ICE HOCKEY

After surviving day one of Dad's new project, *Tryouts for Ben*, I could barely move. Too tired to argue my new hostage status, I climbed into Mom's van without saying a word.

Imagine my surprise when Mom stopped at the mall! As much as I hated shopping, I hoped that was exactly what Mom had in mind today. If she needed to pick up a few things, I'd offer to help. Because shopping sounded better than another sports tryout.

No such luck. I couldn't believe my ears when she said I was there to play ice hockey. I've never skated in my life and skating on ice sounded scary. At this point, I was sure Mom had lost her mind. I didn't think Dad meant for me do anything this crazy. Isn't hockey dangerous?

I stared at my feet and like a condemned man, I followed Mom to the ice rink.

"Listen, Ben, this tryout is just to see if you like hockey. If you do, we'll arrange for some lessons before the season starts. Okay?" Mom said.

I nodded, I mean it's not like I really had a choice.

The coach handed me a helmet, skates, and a hockey stick. The equipment seemed kinda cool.

And after struggling into all of the gear, I had to admit, I looked fierce.

Maybe if I succeeded in moving across the cold, slippery ice on these razor thin skates without breaking a leg, hockey might be fun.

I wobbled over to the team, holding onto the wall as if my life depended on it.

So far so good, that is until…

Just as I'd managed to ease out on the ice, one of the guys raced toward me at the speed of light. He stopped within inches of me, ice shavings flew around my feet. Then the big guy growled at me. He growled! Who does that?

I backed up, stumbled over my skates and slipped on the ice. My first fall. Too bad it wasn't my last.

If you ask me, hockey didn't seem like a very friendly game. It's hard to steer clear of big, growling guys, and chase a tiny little piece of rubber across the ice without falling.

I'm almost embarrassed to tell you what happened. Practice did not go good, not good at all.

I spent more time sitting on the cold, hard ice than skating. For a no tackle game, ice hockey was a dangerous game.

The last time I fell, I landed hard and slid across the ice like a human hockey puck. Talk about embarrassing. My face turned as red as my bottom felt.

When Mom arrived, I let out a big sigh of relief. I limped off the ice and rubbed at the wet seat of my pants. This time, I was sure another important part of my body was broken. Trust me, there's nothing funny about hitting a funny bone. Especially that funny bone.

If you ever decide to play ice hockey, take this tip from me.

Hockey Tip: Wear extra padding in your pants, you'll need it.

After two days of tryouts, I moved like my grandpa, all hunched over, and in slow motion; felt as old, too. At this rate, I may need to borrow his cane.

Although, Alex thought it was cool that I tried out for hockey, he agreed with me.

"You stink," he said. "But this might help with your uh pain." He snickered and tossed me a pillow to sit on. For a big brother, sometimes he's not so bad.

Mom assured me, again, nothing was broken, that I was just sore. Easy for her to say, she's not the one walking funny. I wiggled in my chair and decided a pillow was my new best friend.

Can somebody rescue me, please? Mom's taking me to another tryout tomorrow.

It was going to be a very long summer.

CHAPTER 5 - RUINED BREAKFAST

The next morning, Dad walked in as I was eating a second bowl of cereal. I was starving, tryouts sure make a guy hungry.

"Ben, I'm proud of you for trying out a lot of different sports."

"Uh, thanks, Dad, I think."

"I know you'll soon find one that's just right," he said with a big smile.

Honest, I didn't do it on purpose, it just happened. Cereal shot out of my mouth and landed clear across the table.

What did he mean a lot? How many sports did Dad expect me to try? Find one that's just right? Who did he think I was, Baby Bear or maybe Goldilocks? I'm too big for nursery rhymes.

Parents sure know how to ruin a good breakfast. Milk dripped from my lips as I stared at them.

I looked at the den and my dusty video games. This summer was not working out as I'd planned.

Alex grabbed a pop-tart from the toaster and gave my head an annoying noogie as he passed my chair.

"Have fun, Benji," he called out as he left the room.

"Quit it, and my name is Ben!" I yelled. I hated noogies, and I hated being called Benji. I am not his pet dog. For a big brother, sometimes he's annoying.

Mom motioned to me, "Let's go, she said, "time to check out another sport."

CHAPTER 6 - BASEBALL TRYOUTS

When we arrived at the baseball field, I was relieved to discover no girls. So far so good.

Mom handed me a ball cap. Black, not my favorite color, but whatever. I was too tired to complain about the hat.

"Boys, make feel Ben welcome. He's going to join us today," said the coach.

Most of the players just stared at me, but at least, no one growled.

When the coach shouted, "Okay, Guys, let's play ball!" his voice boomed just like one of the guys on TV.

I grabbed a bat and stepped up to the plate, and thought that baseball might be an okay game, that is until…

I'm almost embarrassed to tell you what happened. Practice did not go good, not good at all.

My first time at the plate, the bat slipped from my hands and flew through the air, as if it had wings. The bat landed with a thud, followed by a scream, as it hit one of the players on his shin.

The coach helped him hobble over to the dugout. What a relief.

If he could limp, that meant his leg wasn't broken, right?

As for me, I went to left field where the coach suggested I practice catching high flies. Not sure what those were, but I agreed to try.

Blinded by the sun, I didn't see the ball. It fell from the sky like a missile aimed straight for my head.

For a no tackle game, baseball sure was a dangerous game. Another sport, another afternoon and I lay on the ground.

When Mom arrived, the coach told her I was okay.

"He stumbled over his own feet and fell," he said, "the ball just knocked off his cap."

Whatever, I had a headache.

Here's a tip you need to remember if you ever want to play baseball.

Baseball Tip: Keep a good grip on the bat and watch out for balls falling from the sky.

That night, Alex pointed out that I was killing off the sports one by one. He had that all wrong, the sports were killing me. Did I mention, I stink at baseball?

"Not many left, Benji," he said.

I gave him my meanest look, wishing I had black greasepaint under my eyes. Maybe I'll ask Mom if she knows where to buy some.

"Leave him alone," said Dad. "I'm proud that Ben keeps trying. You went through the same thing at his age."

"He did?" I asked.

"Yes, he did," Dad said.

I smirked at Alex.

Wow, I stunk and Dad didn't care. I sat up a little straighter.

Sooner or later we'd have to run out of teams to try, right?

I just hoped I'd survive.

CHAPTER 7 - SOCCER FUN

The soccer coach was tall and skinny. I bet, if he tried, he could outrun a cheetah. Have you ever seen a cheetah run? They are the fastest land animal in the world. Cheetahs can run as fast as a car. Now that I think about it, I doubt he could outrun one. But he still looks like a fast runner.

Tryouts started okay and coach seemed nice. None of the kids growled at me and no one had black greasepaint under their eyes. Things were looking up.

Soccer, it turns out, is just another way to play kickball. Everyone runs around chasing each other and the ball, as they try to kick it into a net.

I ran fast but missed the ball more than I kicked it. After a few minutes, I began having fun. I mean, who doesn't like to play chase?

Yeah, I was having fun, that is until….

Well, you guessed it. Practice did not go good, not good at all. I'm almost embarrassed to tell you what happened.

Someone kicked my shin instead of the ball. Not once but a zillion times. Soon I felt my legs turning black and blue.

Then all of a sudden, we collided. Everyone landed in a large pile. And who was on the bottom? Me, that's who. There I lay on the ground under the entire soccer team.

For a no tackle game, soccer sure was a dangerous game.

If you want to try soccer, this tip might help.

Soccer Tip. Try not to land at the bottom of a pile-up, wear tough shoes and shin guards.

After soccer practice, I spent a couple of days playing video games and letting my bruises heal. I don't care what Mom says, this time I'm sure my big toe is broken.

It was going to be a very long summer.

CHAPTER 8 - BASKETBALL GIANT

Monday arrived all too soon, and I found myself at the community center gym. At least playing in an air-conditioned gym sounded better than sweating on another ballfield. An indoor sport can't be too bad, can it?

The gym wasn't freezing cold or blazing hot, but just right. Uh, oh, I shook my head and chased three bears from my mind.

The coach walked over and welcomed me to the eight-year-old boy's league. All right! No girls! No growling and no greasepaint! So far so good.

Turned out, bouncing the basketball on the floor wasn't hard. Didn't take too long and soon I had the hang of dribbling.

Yeah, I could dribble the ball.

But scoring was a lot harder than bouncing the ball up and down.

The basketball hoop might as well have been on Mars. No matter how hard I tried, I never once hit the net. No way, I'd ever score.

Finally, the coach told us to work on passing the ball back and forth. I thought tryouts were going pretty well, that is until….

I'm almost embarrassed to tell you what happened. Practice did not go good, not good at all. The last thing I remember was a ball coming straight at my head.

Bonk! It hit my forehead, and I hit the floor. For a no tackle game, basketball sure was a dangerous game.

Think you want to play basketball? Then take this tip from me.

Basketball Tip: Duck!

I groaned, opened my eyes, stood up, and came face to face with a giant. Well, not actually face to face, more like my face to his shirt.

"You okay, kid?" he asked.

I just nodded. I mean, what do you say to a giant?

With a hand as big as my face, he checked my head for bumps. The coach motioned all the kids back and then went to call my mom.

"You sure you're alright?" the giant asked again, his voice deep and rumbling. Whoa, he sounded just like Darth Vader in the Star Wars movie.

Everyone was staring.

I hung my head and answered, "Yeah, I'm okay, but…."

"But what?" he asked.

"I stink," I said.

"What do you mean?"

"At sports, I stink at sports. I've tried them all. Baseball, soccer, and even hockey."

I blinked back tears and refused to cry even though my head hurt. No one wants to cry in front of a bunch of kids and a giant.

"In the beginning, everybody stinks," said the giant. "But, a team needs players who try hard. If you've tried all those sports, you're that kind of player. A player that doesn't quit."

"But I never do anything right."

I sniffed and wiped my nose on my tee-shirt.

"One day you will. Just remember, it takes work."

He looked at the door. "I think your mom's here."

Yep, the scared looking woman, rushing across the gym, was my mom. You'd think by now, she'd be used to me getting hurt. But like most moms, she panics every time.

The giant smiled. "He's a tough little guy, bounced back up like a pro," he said.

Mom thanked him and the coach for watching over me and said it was time to go home. Tears still threatened to leak from my eyes. Man oh man, I was so ready to leave.

All of a sudden, I was surrounded. The other boys bounced questions at me like ping-pong balls.

"How do you know him?" a redheaded kid asked.

"Huh? Know who?" I was confused.

"Is he your friend?" asked a tall boy with glasses.

"Think he'll be here next week?"

I was clueless. What they were talking about? Did I damage my brain after it bounced off the tile like one of the basketballs?

At last, the redheaded kid explained.

"Man, he's a famous player," he said. "That guy plays on a pro team."

So, turns out the big man wasn't a real giant after all. Guess I should've watched more basketball on TV.

Some of the players pounded my back, others reached for fist bumps and high fives. They treated me like a celebrity. It seems knowing a basketball legend makes a guy popular. None of them laughed, teased or growled at me. In fact, these guys wanted me to come back next week.

Wow! I couldn't wait to get home and tell Dad and Alex. Although, Dad's project to find me a sport wasn't over, I was warming to the idea.

I wasn't sure which one to pick yet. But this time, I'm not embarrassed to tell you what happened. Practice wasn't too bad, not too bad at all.

Maybe playing on a team might be fun. That girl on the baseball team was kind of nice. She didn't growl or hit me with a ball.

I did look fierce in that hockey uniform, and I ran faster than some of the other players on the soccer field. Yeah, joining a team might not be bad, not bad at all.

Besides, maybe Mr. Giant was right, maybe everyone stinks in the beginning. But not everyone gets to meet a famous player. I think this might turn out to be a great summer after all.

ABOUT THE AUTHOR

Jean M. Cogdell grew up in a small SC town, located near the Great Smoky Mountains. Her short stories and essays have been published in numerous online magazines and journals. You can read more about her writing and life on her blog, jeanswriting.com. Also, connect with her through social media on Twitter @jeancogdell and on Facebook.com/jean.cogdell. Jean currently resides in Sachse, TX.

www.ingramcontent.com/pod-product-compliance
Lightning Source LLC
Chambersburg PA
CBHW040331300426
44113CB00020B/2721